LITTLE IRISH
HISTORY
HEROES
Niamh Donnellan
ILLUSTRATED BY Brian Fitzgerald
GILL BOOKS

For Ann and Pat – N.D

Gill Books
Hume Avenue
Park West
Dublin 12
www.gillbooks.ie

Gill Books is an imprint of M.H. Gill and Co.

978 18045 8356 2

Designed by Bex Sheridan
Printed and bound by L.E.G.O. SpA, Italy
This book is typeset in 16 on 24pt, Quasimoda.

The paper used in this book comes from the wood pulp of sustainably managed forests.

A CIP catalogue record for this book is available from the British Library.

5 4 3 2 1

CONTENTS

FIONN MAC CUMHAILL

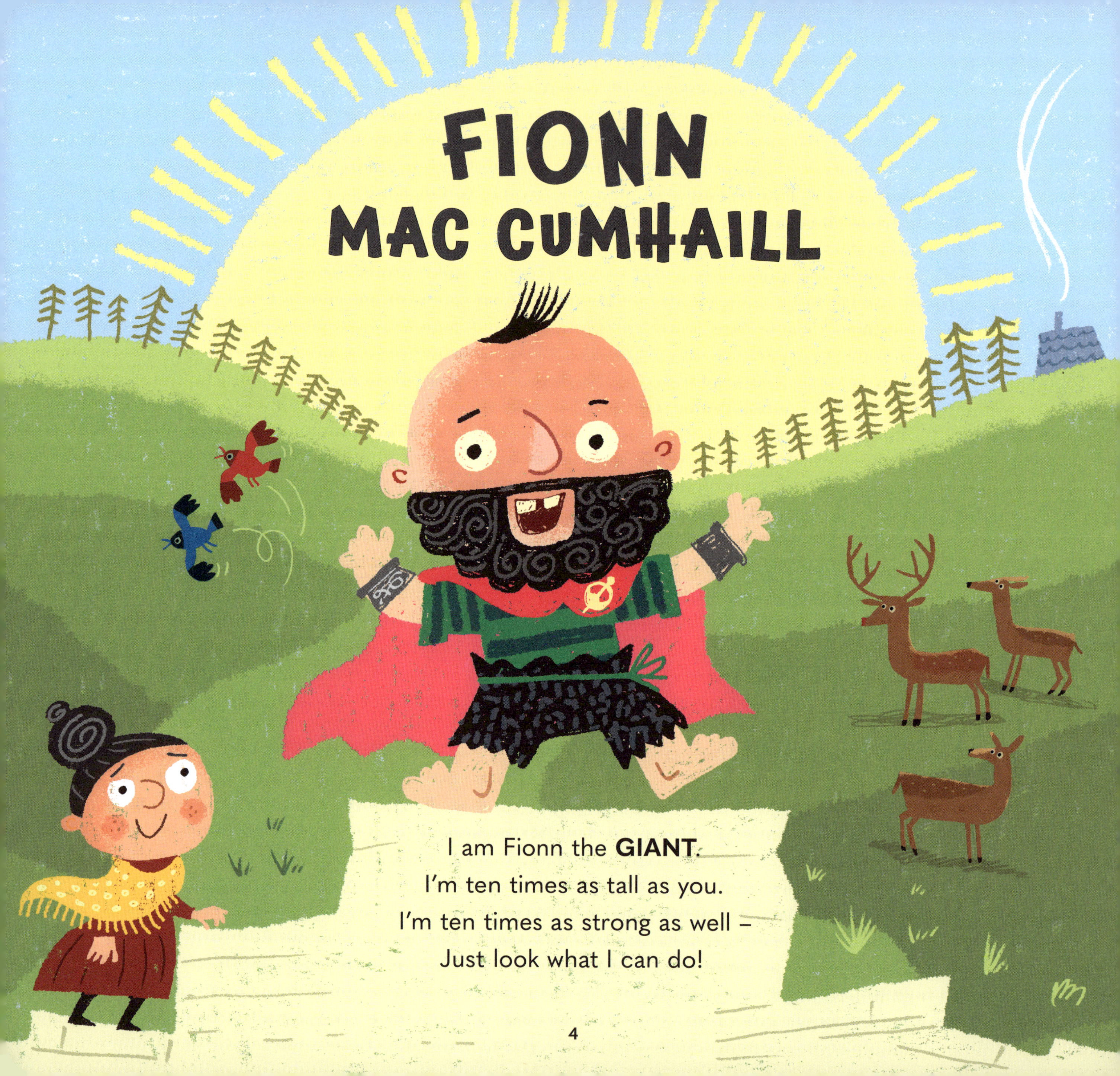

I am Fionn the **GIANT**.
I'm ten times as tall as you.
I'm ten times as strong as well –
Just look what I can do!

I can lift a tree out from the ground
And **THROW** it like a spear.
I can jump over a mountain
To get from there to here.

I know another giant,
Benandonner is his name.
He lives over the sea in Scotland
And **DESTRUCTION** is his game.

My plan was to fight him,
To stop his evil deeds.
But first I had to find a way
To cross those deep, dark seas.

So, I stood on the coast
And threw big boulders in the water.
One, two, three ...
TEN THOUSAND!
My strength, it did not falter.

Soon my path of stones
Reached almost out of sight.
I strode across to Scotland,
But then I got a **FRIGHT**!

I saw the Scottish giant
Before he could spy me.
And oh! – he was the biggest man
That I had ever seen!

His feet were big as hay bales.
His legs were thick as trees.
His hands were like huge branches.
Beside him, birds looked like bees.

I took one look at him
And knew I needed a new plan.
So I hurried home to Ireland;
I ran and ran and ran.

Soon the giant saw my causeway
And set out with a frown.
He stomped right up to my front door
And nearly **KNOCKED** it down.

'WHERE IS FIONN?' he shouted,
In a voice as loud as thunder.
'Come out and **FIGHT**, you coward!
Or I'll tear your house asunder.'

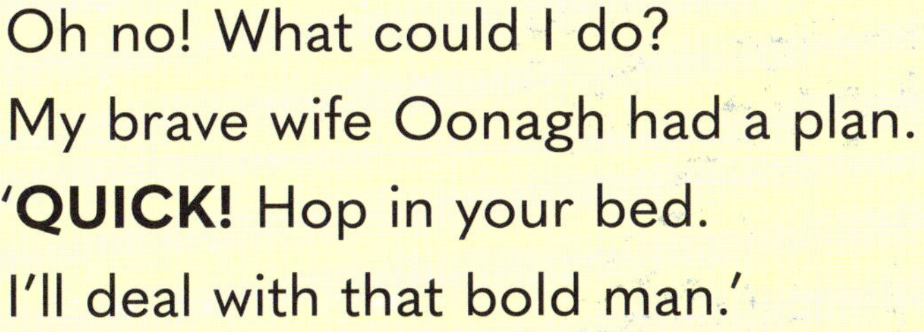

Oh no! What could I do?
My brave wife Oonagh had a plan.
'**QUICK!** Hop in your bed.
I'll deal with that bold man.'

She opened up the door,
And cool as cool can be,
She said, 'Come in, Benandonner.
Sit down and have some tea.'

'Fionn isn't here right now.
I'm sure he'll be back soon.
It's just me and the baby,
Asleep in the next room.'

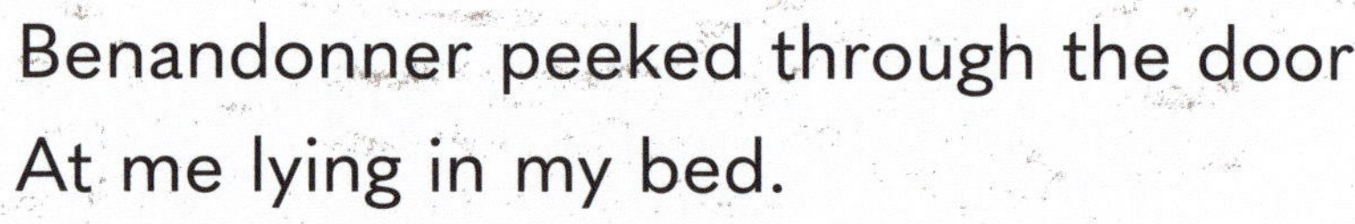

Benandonner peeked through the door
At me lying in my bed.
'THAT'S THE BABY?!' he exclaimed,
Scratching his big head.

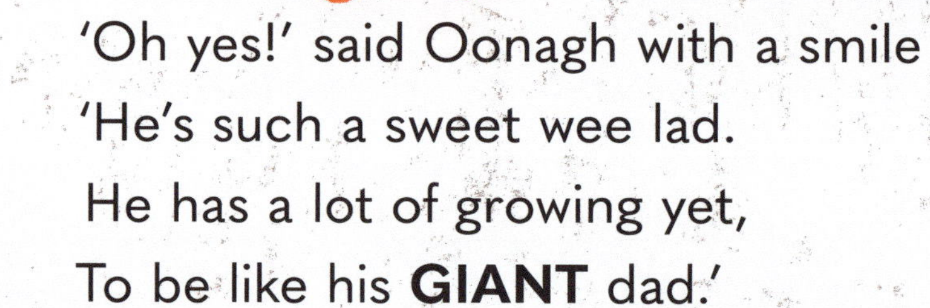

'Oh yes!' said Oonagh with a smile
'He's such a sweet wee lad.
He has a lot of growing yet,
To be like his **GIANT** dad.'

'That baby has a beard!' he gulped.
His face turned white as snow.
'I'm sorry for disturbing you.
I think I'd better go.'

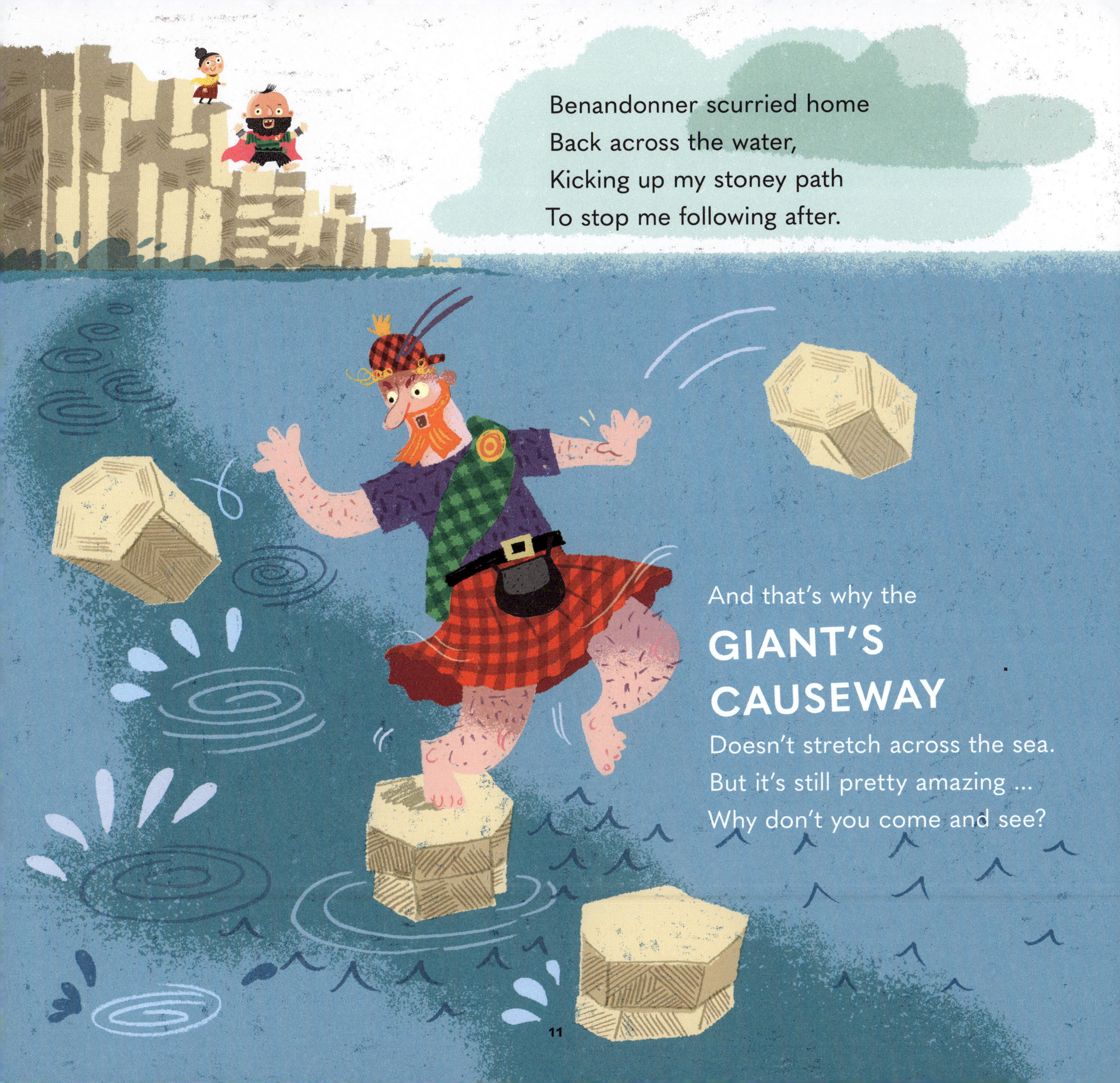

Benandonner scurried home
Back across the water,
Kicking up my stoney path
To stop me following after.

And that's why the

GIANT'S CAUSEWAY

Doesn't stretch across the sea.
But it's still pretty amazing ...
Why don't you come and see?

GRACE O'MALLEY

I am Grace, the Pirate Queen
From the fine county of Mayo.
Are you ready for **ADVENTURE**?
Hop aboard! Let's go!

Some call me Gráinne Mhaol.
You may well wonder why.
It means 'bald Grace' in English
And it's a nickname I go by.

When I was very young
My father said to me
'Your long hair will get in the way
If I take you out to sea!'

But that wasn't going to stop me,
So I chopped my lovely hair.
My father said,
'YOU SCALLYWAG!'
He didn't think I'd dare.

But he was a fair man,
So he welcomed me on board.
I climbed straight to the crow's nest.
'I'M A PIRATE NOW!' I roared.

My ship she is a beauty,
Sleek and strong and fast.
I love every part of her,
From the anchor to the mast.

With my loyal pirate crew
I sail the wild Atlantic sea.
We seek out adventures
Wherever they may be.

Meet Patch, the one-eyed pirate,
And Hoppy, with one leg.
Chef Scurvy cooks our meals,
And for washing, talk to Peg.

They're a very jolly lot,
Singing sea shanties all day long.
When I'm not scanning the horizon
I join in with a song.

Aha! We spy a lonely boat.
My crew spring into place.
'LET'S DO SOME PIRATING!' I shout.
A grin upon my face.

We chase the boat across the water.
There's nowhere for them to hide.
Our ship cuts through the waves like silk.
Soon we're side by side.

We jump aboard the boat
And take everything we can.
Gold and silver, gems and pearls,
Ten pots of strawberry jam!

Two cows, five hens, a wheel of cheese,
A pretty paper kite,
One hundred juicy oranges –
We'll eat like **KINGS** tonight!

Back in my big castle
I share out all the treasure.
Each pirate gets their loot
To enjoy at their leisure.

You could call us naughty,
And you'd probably be right.
I wouldn't recommend this life
On a dark and **STORMY** night.

There are storms at sea so violent
We're **TOSSED** and **THROWN** about.
Huge waves **CRASH** across the deck.
The wind whips away our shouts.

But on a sunny summer's day
When I dive down from the boat –
SPLASH!
– into the shining water,
I swim and dream and float.

I met the Queen of England once,
Dressed in her finery.
But I wouldn't swap all of her jewels
For my **DARING** life at sea.

CÚ CHULAINN

I am the great Cú Chulainn.
And since I was very small
I've been the strongest, fastest,
SMARTEST warrior of all.

At four, I could run quicker
Than a galloping racehorse.
At six, I hit a sliotar
With **EXTRAORDINARY** force.

You might know me as Setanta –
That used to be my name.
But after Culann's party
Things were never quite the same.

I went to the party with my uncle,
Conor, the wise King.
He walked on ahead
While I was dawdling.

I was hurling in the garden
And forgot about the time.
Everyone else went inside
And locked the doors behind.

I saw that it was getting late
And rushed to Culann's door.
But as I hurried up the path
I heard a fearsome roar.

Culann unchained his wolfhound
To guard his house from danger.
But little did I know,
His dog would think I was a stranger.

Culann's dog ran towards me!
He was a scary beast:
His paws were big as dinner plates,
He weighed ten stone at least.

The dog barked and growled,
The hair raised on his back.
He looked like he was hungry …
And I was his next snack!

I took my hurley in my hand,
And picked my sliotar up.
I **WHACKED** the ball with all my strength
Straight at that snarling pup.

The dog was hit! He howled in pain,
And lay down in the dirt.
King Conor rushed out from the house –
He thought that I was hurt.

He looked at me in wonder,
And before I could explain,
The beast got up and **RAN** away
And was **NEVER** seen again.

Culann was upset
That his guard dog had retired.
I said I'd take his place.
Culann said, 'you're hired!'

So, I became the hound of Culann,
'CÚ CHULAINN!' they all shout.
Now I protect the whole of Ulster,
And help everybody out.

QUEEN MAEVE

Hello, my little rascals!
I'm Queen Maeve from the West.
I am a **FEARSOME** warrior –
Some say I am quite the best.

I've stolen many wondrous things,
Gold crowns and splendid jewellery.
But there's one more thing that I desire:
The **BOLD BROWN BULL** of Cooley.

This bull is quite magnificent,
The **STRONGEST** in the land.
His eyes flash bright like rubies,
He could **BITE** off a man's **HAND**.

I sent my men to speak to Daire,
The owner of this **BEAST**,
To ask if I could borrow him
For a year or two at least.

When Daire said, 'no thanks'
I shouted, stomped, and stormed.
'**NOBODY** says no to me!
I'll get you! You've been warned!'

We marched to Daire's home.
I was sure that we would win
But on the way we met
The great warrior Cú Chulainn.

He battled many of my men
And won every single fight.
Every day more were defeated,
Or ran home through the night.

Eventually no one was left,
So it was up to me
To raid Daire's home and grab my prize,
The great brown Bull of Cooley.

I dragged that wondrous beast
All the way back home
To a big field full of **TASTY GRASS**,
Where he was free to roam.

But the bull was very angry:
He ran right through the gate,
Then **CHARGED** at my castle doors.
Things were not looking great.

He **STOMPED** into the kitchens
And **SMASHED** all of my dishes.
He **SPLASHED** around my lake
And frightened all the **FISHES**.

I tried to stop his rampage
But he was very strong.
I chased him **ROUND** and **ROUND**
All day and all night long.

Finally I caught him
And looked straight into his eyes.

'STOP YOUR MESSING, BULL!'

I said.

He looked quite surprised.

'Now, will you please behave yourself?'
The bull gave a quiet moo.
Then I looked down and saw
A giant **COWPAT** on my shoe!

That was the final straw!
I set that brown bull free.
He ran **STRAIGHT** home to Daire
Where he lived quite happily.

I wish I'd never taken him
That bull was so, so bold.
And I have learned my lesson:
I'll stick with stealing gold!

ST BRIGID

Hello, my name is Brigid.
I'm a saint and an abbess,
Known all over Ireland –
To some I'm a **GODDESS**.

When I was a little girl,
I did many caring things.
I gave food to hungry people
and mended **BROKEN** wings.

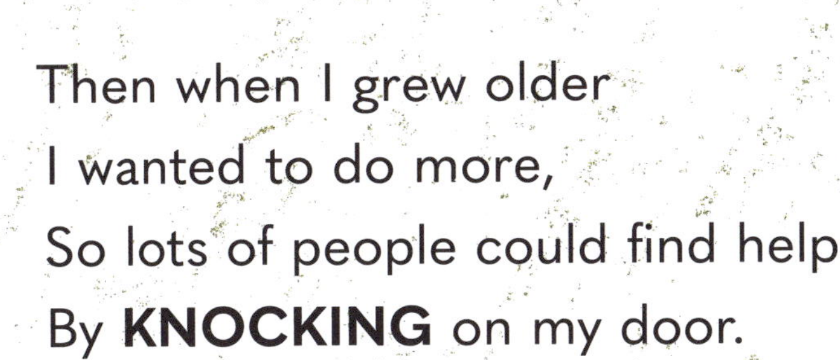

Then when I grew older
I wanted to do more,
So lots of people could find help
By **KNOCKING** on my door.

I decided to build a monastery,
A place of peace and joy,
Where there was food and comfort
For every girl and boy.

I went looking for a field
To build my fine abbey.
Finally, I found a spot
That suited brilliantly!

It was near a leafy forest,
Full of wood to chop.
The land was rich and green
So we could grow our crops.

There was a big lake too,
Full of fresh water to drink –
A fine place to swim on summer days.
Sounds perfect, don't you think?

The king of Leinster owned the land
So I told him of my plan.
He said, 'No, not a chance!'
He was a stubborn man.

I asked him once again.
I gave it one last shot.
'Give me all the land my cloak can cover.'
He laughed, 'That's not a lot!'

I took my cloak from round my neck
And threw it in the air.
It sparkled and it shone
As everybody stared.

The cloak grew and **GREW** and **GREW**,
Until it covered all the land
From the forest to the lake.
It really did look grand.

The king was quite astonished.
He could not believe his eyes.
He said I could have his field,
And even gave me some supplies.

I gathered round my friends,
We worked all day and night.
Digging, hammering and sawing
Until it was **JUST RIGHT**.

I sat down by my new front door
And saw the morning sun shine gold.
The world was **WAKING UP**
After a winter long and cold.

All my dreams had come true,
I'd built my **MONASTERY!**
It was the first of February –
A special day for me.

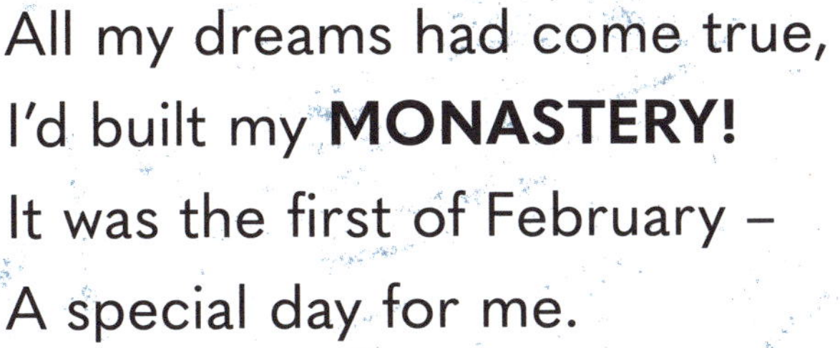

Now they call it St Brigid's Day,
And it marks the start of Spring.
It's a time to celebrate,
To laugh and dance and sing!

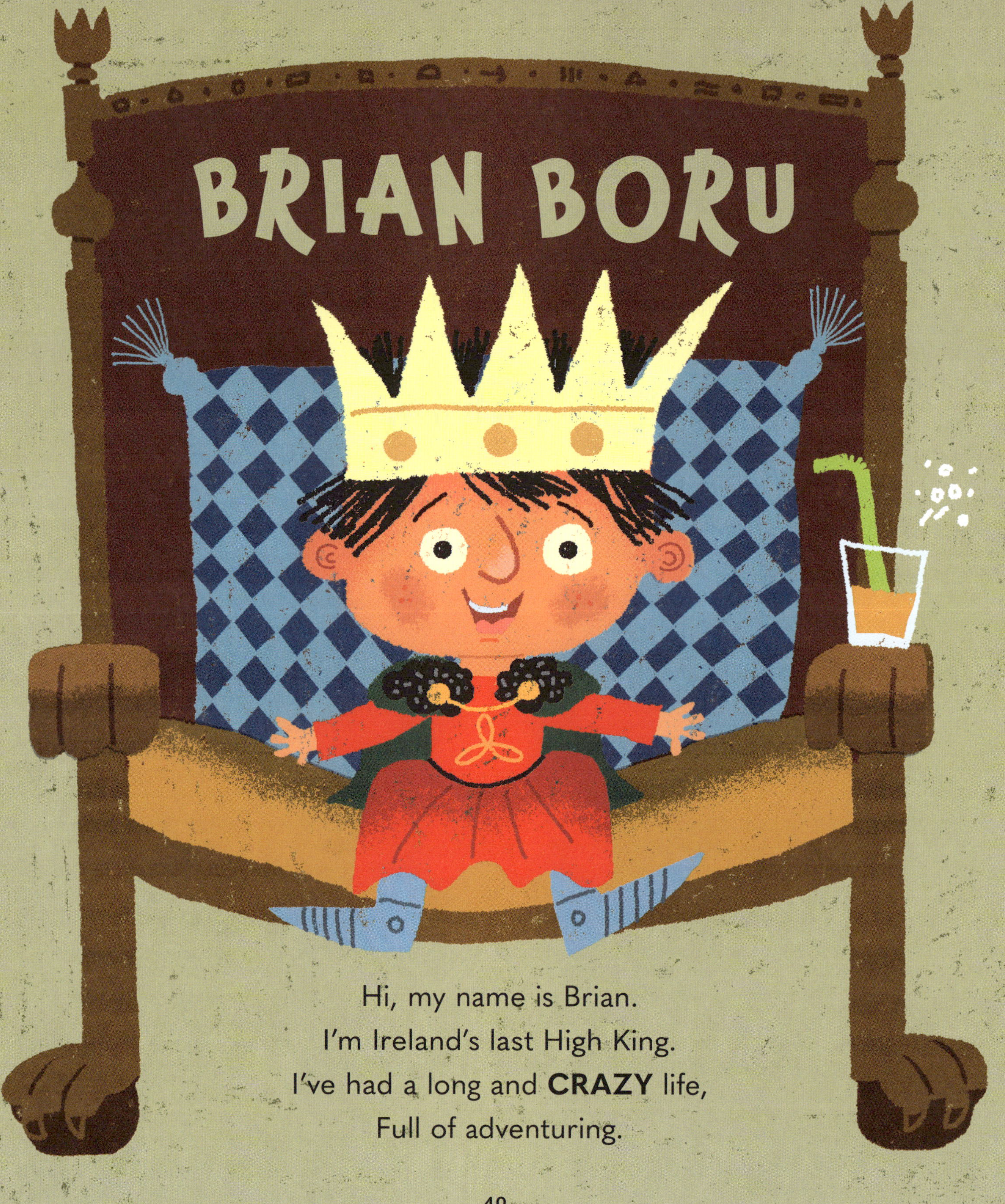

BRIAN BORU

Hi, my name is Brian.
I'm Ireland's last High King.
I've had a long and **CRAZY** life,
Full of adventuring.

I am the youngest of twelve brothers,
Who all pushed me around.
So, since I was very little,
I've learned to **STAND** my ground.

I'm big and strong and brave now,
Like all the men from County Clare.
When **PEOPLE** see me coming,
They throw their **HATS** up in the air!

Would you like to hear the tale
Of the biggest fight I've seen?
It was the Battle of Clontarf
In the year 1014.

I ruled over most of Ireland,
Except for Dublin town.
There, Sitric Silkbeard was in charge –
Until I took him down!

Sitric was a Viking,
And my fiercest enemy.
He rounded up an army
That came by land and sea.

I gathered my men too.
We marched all day and night
To Clontarf where we set up camp,
And prepared to join the fight.

We were woken up at dawn
By the sound of **BATTLE DRUMS.**
They echoed across Dublin Bay.
The Viking **SHIPS** had come!

Sailing through the sea mist,
They were a **FEARSOME** sight.
Longboats full of **WARRIORS**
Ready for the fight.

Each boat had a wooden dragon's head
That loomed out of the fog.
But my men were never scared
For we had our wolfhound dogs.

Have you heard the Clare shout?
Some call it the banner **ROAR**.
It's a mighty fearsome yell
That will **SHAKE** you to the core.

Well, that's what the Vikings heard,
As they sailed into the bay.
I'm surprised they didn't turn around
And **GO HOME** straight away!

Each Viking had a helmet
And an axe of a good size.
They charged towards our army
With **FIRE** glowing in their eyes.

We threw our spears so far
They rained down from the sky.
The Vikings held their wooden **SHIELDS**
And **LIFTED** them up high.

We fought the Vikings valiantly
With our trusty **IRON SPEARS**.
And in the end, my army won.
But not without some tears.

Ireland's a **GREAT** country
Of that there is no doubt.
Do you agree with me?
Then yell a loud Clare **SHOUT!**

NIAMH DONNELLAN is a writer and poet, and the author of *Little Irish Folklore Friends*, also published by Gill Books. She lives in Kilkenny with her family and two mischievous cats.

BRIAN FITZGERALD is an author and illustrator of children's picture books. He is the winner of the International Silent Book Competition at Bologna, The White Raven Award, Gradam Réics Carló and the CLÉ Children's Book of the Year Award 2025. His work was included in the US Kindergarten curriculum in 2025. Brian lives and works in Dún Laoghaire.